HOLIDAYS, FESTIVALS, & CELEBRATIONS

INDEPENDENCE DAY

BY ANN HEINRICHS · ILLUSTRATED BY ROBERT SQUIER

J 394.2634
Heinrichs

The Child's World

Published in the United States of America by The Child's World®
PO Box 326 • Chanhassen, MN 55317-0326
800-599-READ • www.childsworld.com

ACKNOWLEDGMENTS
The Child's World®: Mary Berendes, Publishing Director

Editorial Directions, Inc.: E. Russell Primm, Editorial Director; Katie Marsico, Managing Editor; Judith Shiffer, Assistant Editor; Caroline Wood and Rory Mabin, Editorial Assistants; Susan Hindman, Copy Editor and Proofreader; Elizabeth Nellums, Rory Mabin, Ruth Martin, and Caroline Wood, Fact Checkers; Tim Griffin/ IndexServ, Indexer

The Design Lab: Kathleen Petelinsek, Design and Page Production

LIBRARY OF CONGRESS CATALOGING-IN-PUBLICATION DATA
Heinrichs, Ann.
  Independence Day / written by Ann Heinrichs ; illustrated by Robert Squier.
    p. cm. — (Holidays, festivals, & celebrations)
  Includes index.
  ISBN 1-59296-577-6 (library bound : alk. paper)
  1. Fourth of July—Juvenile literature. 2. Fourth of July celebrations—Juvenile literature. I. Squier, Robert, ill.
II. Title. III. Series.
  E286.A1353 2006
  394.2634—dc22   2005025684

TABLE OF CONTENTS

CHAPTER ONE

HAPPY BIRTHDAY, AMERICA!

Firecrackers crackle and pop. Flags are waving. Bands march down the street. Yummy food sizzles on the **grill**. And fireworks light up the sky. It's **Independence** Day!

Independence Day is also called the Fourth of July. It's like a big birthday party. Who's having a birthday that day? The United States!

Americans celebrate their freedom that day. They show their love for their country. They're proud to live in a free land!

Cooking food on the grill is a popular Independence Day activity.

CHAPTER TWO

FIGHTING FOR FREEDOM

Today, the United States has fifty states. But the country used to be much smaller. It began with only thirteen states. Those states were once **colonies.** They belonged to Great Britain. The colonies didn't like British rule. They wanted to be free. So they fought for their freedom. That fight was the Revolutionary War.

Colonists fought hard for freedom from British rule.

The Revolutionary War began in 1775. The last battle was fought in 1781.

Give me liberty or give
me death!
—*Patrick Henry*
(1736–1799)

CHAPTER THREE

SAYING IT IN WRITING

The colonies' leaders formed a **congress**. They met in Philadelphia, Pennsylvania. They planned to write a **Declaration** of Independence. It would explain why they wanted to be free.

Colonial leaders met in Philadelphia to write the Declaration of Independence.

Ask not what your country can do for you— ask what you can do for your country.
—John F. Kennedy (1917–1963), thirty-fifth president

We ... do ... declare, that these United Colonies are ... free and Independent States ...
—From the Declaration of Independence

Thomas Jefferson was the main writer. He worked for days. He wrote that all people are equal. They had the right to be free. And they should rule themselves. The colonies, he said, should be free states.

Members of the congress liked what Jefferson wrote. They voted yes on July 4, 1776. We call that Independence Day. At last, the colonies won the war. They became the United States of America!

Thomas Jefferson became the third U.S. president.

Thomas Jefferson was the main writer to work on the Declaration of Independence.

CHAPTER FOUR

A GRAND BIRTHDAY PARTY

Bells rang in one city after another. People gathered in city squares. What was all the fuss about? The Declaration of Independence was being read. Oh, how people cheered!

Crowds cheered to hear the Declaration of Independence read.

July 4, 1777, was the country's first birthday. Philadelphia had a grand party that day. Ships lined up in the **harbor**. They were decked out in red, white, and blue. The ships fired thirteen cannons. That was one for each new state. Soldiers marched in a parade. And fireworks flashed across the sky.

More than two hundred years have passed since then. But we still celebrate the Fourth of July. That's how we say "Happy birthday, America!"

Philadelphia hosted a colorful Independence Day celebration in 1777.

THE FLAG GOES BY

Hats off!

Along the street there comes

A blare of bugles,

  a ruffle of drums,

And loyal hearts are

  beating high:

Hats off!

The flag is passing by!

—Henry Holcomb Bennett

  (1863–1924)

CHAPTER FIVE

FLAGS, PARADES, AND MUSIC

You know when it's Independence Day. Just look around! American flags are waving. Homes and shops display them proudly. Decorations are red, white, and blue. They match the colors of the flag.

Parades that day are noisy and colorful. Floats and marching bands go by. The crowds wave flags and cheer. Soldiers often join the parade. They are proud to serve their country.

It's a great day for music, too. Bands play **patriotic** tunes. People like to sing along to their favorites. They're proud of their country!

U.S. soldiers often march in Independence Day parades.

AMERICA THE BEAUTIFUL

O beautiful for spacious skies,
For amber waves of grain,
For purple mountain majesties
Above the fruited plain!
America! America! God
shed his grace on thee
And crown thy good with
brotherhood
From sea to shining sea!
—Katherine Lee Bates
(1859–1929)

CHAPTER SIX

A DAY IN THE PARK

Many families have picnics on Independence Day. They might go to a city park or even a friend's backyard. There they fire up a grill. Soon hamburgers and hot dogs are sizzling. Ears of corn are roasting. There are big pots of potato salad and baked beans. And for dessert? A nice, juicy watermelon or an apple pie!

As night falls, the show begins. Blazing fireworks light up the sky. Streaming rockets and bursting stars—yahoo! What a perfect Fourth of July!

Watching a fireworks display is the perfect way to wrap up Independence Day celebrations.

THE AMERICAN FLAG

As red as a fire,
As blue as the sky,
As white as the snow—
See our flag fly!
Three pretty colors
Wave at the sky,
Red, white and blue
On the Fourth of July!

Red, white and blue
Those colors are,
And every state has
Its very own star.
Hold up the flag,
Hold it up high,
And then say, "Hurrah,
For the Fourth of July!"
—Author unknown

CHAPTER SEVEN

SOME FAVORITE SONGS

America

My country, 'tis of thee,
Sweet land of liberty,
Of thee I sing.
Land where my fathers died!
Land of the Pilgrims' pride!
From every mountain side
Let freedom ring!

—Samuel F. Smith
(1808–1895)

Yankee Doodle

Yankee Doodle went to town
A-riding on a pony.
Stuck a feather in his hat
And called it macaroni.

Yankee Doodle, keep it up,
Yankee Doodle dandy,
Mind the music and the step
And with the girls be handy.

—Author unknown

Colonists sang "Yankee Doodle"
during the Revolutionary War.

I'm a Yankee Doodle Dandy

I'm a Yankee Doodle Dandy,
A Yankee Doodle, do or die;
A real live nephew of my Uncle Sam's,
Born on the Fourth of July.

I've got a Yankee Doodle sweetheart
She's my Yankee Doodle joy.
Yankee Doodle came to London
Just to ride the ponies;
I am a Yankee Doodle boy.

—George M. Cohan
(1878–1942)

Independence Day

CHAPTER EIGHT

DID YOU KNOW?

- John Adams was the second president. Thomas Jefferson was the third president. Both men died on July 4, 1826. That was the country's fiftieth birthday!
- James Monroe was the fifth president. He died on July 4, 1831.
- Calvin Coolidge was the thirtieth president. He was born on July 4, 1872.
- The American flag has thirteen red and white stripes. They stand for the thirteen colonies.
- Washington, D.C., is the nation's capital. It holds the country's most famous fireworks display. The fireworks go off on the National Mall.

Joining in the Spirit of Independence Day

· Find some pictures that show life during Revolutionary War times. Draw a picture of yourself as you would look then.

· Does your city hold an Independence Day parade? If so, name some groups that march in the parade. How do they show their feelings for their country?

· Veterans are people who have fought in wars. Is there a veterans' hospital in your community? If so, visit the veterans. Ask them about their lives. Thank them for serving their country.

· Do you know someone from another country? Ask how his or her country celebrates its independence.

Making Patriotic Fruit Salad

Ingredients:
1 cup strawberries (sliced)
1 cup blueberries
1 cup raspberries
1 cup bananas (sliced)
1 ½ cups vanilla yogurt

Directions:
Rinse the strawberries, blueberries, and raspberries under cold water. Carefully slice the bananas and strawberries into smaller pieces.* (Depending on your favorite fruit, you can use more or less of any ingredient!) Mix all the fruit together in a large bowl, and stir in the vanilla yogurt. Share your salad at an Independence Day picnic—it should serve about eight people!

Have an adult help you use a knife to slice the fruit.

Making a Flag Fan
*Show off your patriotism and keep cool at
the same time with this fun project.*

What you need:
1 large sheet of white paper
Red and blue markers
Pencil
Ruler
Scotch tape

Instructions:
1. Place the paper on the table horizontally (lengthwise, like a flag).
2. Use your pencil to draw a rectangle in the upper left corner of the flag.
3. Draw a bunch of stars with your pencil inside the rectangle.
4. Color around the stars inside the rectangle with the blue marker. Leave the stars white.
5. Use your pencil and ruler to draw horizontal stripes on the rest of your paper.
6. Color in every other stripe with the red marker. Leave the rest of the stripes white.
7. Fold the flag accordion style from left to right.
8. Hold the fan closed and tape about 1 inch of the flag together at the bottom.

Now you're ready to watch a parade or fireworks display in style.
Happy Independence Day!

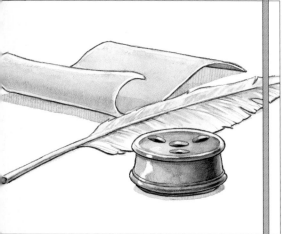

Words to Know

colonies *(KOL-uh-neez)* lands with ties to a mother country

congress *(KON-gruss)* a group of people who meet and speak for others

declaration *(dek-luh-RAY-shun)* the act of announcing something

grill *(GRILL)* a cooking stove with bars above the flames

harbor *(HAR-burr)* a place where ships can come up to the shore

independence *(in-dee-PEN-dens)* freedom from rule by others

patriotic *(pay-tree-AH-tik)* showing love for one's country

How to Learn More about Independence Day

At the Library

McDonald, Megan, and Peter H. Reynolds (illustrator). *Judy Moody Declares Independence.* Cambridge, Mass.: Candlewick Press, 2005.

Osborne, Mary Pope, and Peter Catalanotto. *Happy Birthday, America.* Brookfield, Conn.: Roaring Brook Press, 2003.

Rockwell, Anne, and Cynthia von Buhler. *They Called Her Molly Pitcher.* New York: Alfred A. Knopf, 2002.

Wong, Janet S., and Margaret Chodos-Irvine. *Apple Pie 4th of July.* San Diego: Harcourt, 2002.

On the Web

Visit our home page for lots of links about Independence Day:
http://www.childsworld.com/links
NOTE TO PARENTS, TEACHERS, AND LIBRARIANS:
We routinely verify our Web links to make sure they're safe,
active sites—so encourage your readers to check them out!

ABOUT THE AUTHOR

Ann Heinrichs lives in Chicago, Illinois. She has written more than two hundred books for children. She loves traveling to faraway places.

ABOUT THE ILLUSTRATOR

Robert Squier loves to illustrate stories using watercolor, ink, and colored pencils. When he's not drawing in Portsmouth, New Hampshire, you can find him ballroom dancing or camping.

Index